KB265056

# The Golden Bird

Little Storyteller
# The Golden Bird  황금새

저자 Carla Schmitz

초판 1쇄 인쇄 2011년 7월 11일     초판 1쇄 발행 2011년 7월 18일

발행인 박효상     책임 편집 강성실     편집·진행 모희진     영업 이종선 · 이태호 · 이전희
기획 이희경     디자인 장선숙     삽화 이창준

출판등록 제 10-1835호     발행처 사람in     주소 121-839 서울시 마포구 서교동 378-16 강화빌딩 4F
전화 02)338-3555(代)     팩스 02)338-3545(代)     E-mail saramin@netsgo.com     Homepage www.saramin.com

※ 책값은 뒤표지에 있습니다.     ※ 파본은 바꾸어 드립니다.

ⓒ Saramin 2011

ISBN  978-89-6049-256-1 18740     978-89-6049-211-0(set)

# The Golden Bird

written by **Brothers Grimm**    rewritten by **Carla Schmitz**    illustrated by **Changjoon Lee**    narrated by **Anna Grant**

## Story

본문에 표기되어 있는 끊어 읽기(✔)와 강세(●) 표시를 보면서
오디오를 듣고 스토리텔링해보세요.

## Word Study & Key Expression

이야기를 이해하는 데 필수적으로 알아야 할 핵심 어휘와
표현입니다. 어휘와 표현의 해석과 해설은 사람in 홈페이지에서
보충학습 자료로 별도로 제공됩니다.

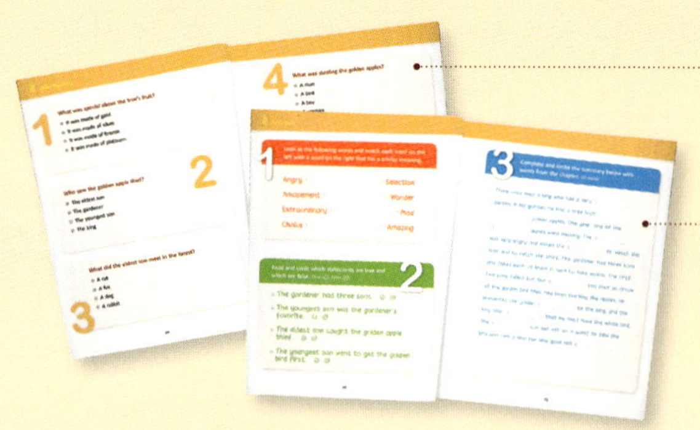

## After Reading

각 챕터를 읽고 난 후 퀴즈를 통해
이해력을 측정해 봅니다.

## Activities

각 챕터의 내용을 바탕으로
Matching, True or False,
Summary 등의 활동을 해봅니다.

## Reading Diary

이야기를 모두 읽고 난 후 느낀 점과 이야기에 대한
자신의 생각을 간단히 정리해봄으로써
독서 감상문의 뼈대를 만들어봅니다.

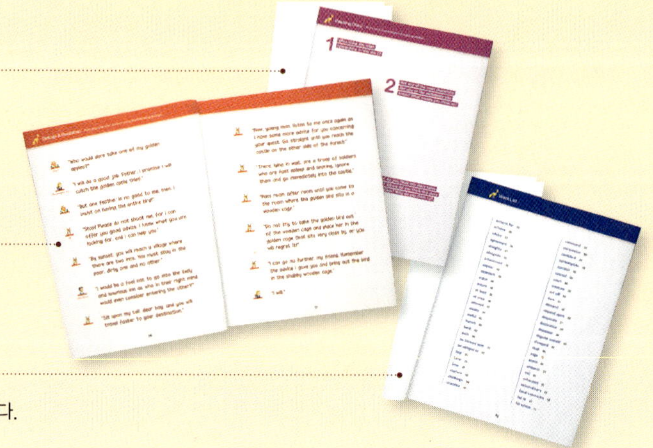

## Dialogs & Recitation

스토리에 나온 대화문만을 모아 역할극(Role Play)에
활용해봅니다.

## Word List

책에 나온 필수 어휘들을 알파벳순으로 정리하였습니다.

### Audio 자료

Storytelling과 Read Along 두 가
지 버전의 MP3 파일이 제공되며
Word Study & Key Expression의
음원도 별도로 제공됩니다.

**www. saramin. com**

### 보충학습자료

스토리 본문, 어휘, Activities의 해석 및 해설
이 담겨 있는 보충학습자료를 사람in 홈페이
지(www.saramin.com)에서 pdf 파일로 다운
로드 받으실 수 있습니다.

# Contents

# The Golden Bird

Once upon a time, a king had a beautiful garden with a very precious tree. It was a tree that produced golden apples each year. On a dark night, one of the golden apples was missing. The king was so upset that he ordered the royal gardener to watch the tree during the night. Although the gardener's three sons failed to capture the thief, the youngest son made a golden bird leave a single feather behind and delivered it to the king. The king insisted on having the entire golden bird, so the gardener's three sons set off the journey to find the golden bird...

Your life would not be spared unless you could bring me a golden horse!
If you could bring me a beautiful princess, I'll give you the golden horse.
I know what you are looking for, boy. I can help you. Just follow my advice, and you will get it!
If you expect to have my daughter easily, don't even think about it!

# The Missing Apples

Once upon a time, a king lived in a beautiful land. The king also had a very beautiful garden, and in this garden stood a very unusual and precious tree. It was a tree that produced golden apples each year. As the tree was worth a lot, each year, as the tree bore its fruit, the apples had to be accounted for each night to make sure none was lost or stolen. However, on a dark night one year, as the time grew closer for the apples to be ripe and to fall from the tree, one of the golden apples went missing.

The king was very angry. "Who would dare take one of my golden apples?" he asked in amazement, but no one came forward.

On the following evening, the king instructed the royal gardener to watch the tree during the night to find out who had taken his golden apple. The gardener, being an older man with three sons, commanded that his eldest son take the first watch. When night fell, the gardener's eldest son went and sat underneath the tree and waited for the thief to show up; however, by the stroke of midnight, the boy had fallen asleep.

As the morning sun awoke the boy beneath the tree, he got up to count the apples while hoping that the same number were still there from the night

**Word Study**

instruct    royal    find out    command    show up    fall asleep    presence    fate
fail to    capture

**Key Expression**

He got up to count the apples ***while hoping*** that the same number were still there from the night before.

before and that his presence alone had kept the thief at bay. Despite his hope though, the eldest son had failed, and another apple was missing.

On the next evening, the gardener sent his second son. He hoped that this son would do a better job than his elder brother. However, their fate was the same. The son on the second night had, like his brother, fallen asleep when the clock struck midnight and had failed to capture the thief of yet another golden apple. Now, three apples had gone missing.

The gardener had a third son, who was his youngest and favorite. His third son had begged his father to let him watch over the golden tree. "I will do a good job, Father. I promise I will catch the golden apple thief," he said to his father over and over again. So he had to allow his third son at least to try.

On the third night, the third son took his place under the tree. The midnight bell rang across the land, but the boy stayed awake. To his surprise, just a short while after midnight, he started to hear a rustling sound as if something were dancing in the leaves. He looked up, and there before him, pecking at the golden apples, was a bird made of pure gold.

As it was snapping at one of the apples, the youngest son stood up and tried to shoot an arrow at the bird. Although this did not capture the bird, it did cause a single feather to fall from its tail and frightened it enough to fly away.

The third son delivered the golden feather to the king in the morning and explained his extraordinary story. The king summoned his council at once, and everyone was in agreement that the feather was worth more than all the wealth in the kingdom.

"But one feather is no good to me, men. I insist on having the entire bird!" the king demanded.

The challenge fell once again to the gardener's sons to fulfill the king's demands. As before, ignoring the pleas of his youngest son, the gardener sent his eldest son out to find the golden bird. The eldest, despite his initial failure, set off confident

**Word Study**

extraordinary    summon    council    at once    agreement    demand    plea    initial
set off    entrance    bow    attempt    get ready to    offer    advice

**Key Expression**

As before, *ignoring* the pleas of his youngest son, the gardener sent his eldest son out to find the golden bird.

as he was sure that he, the oldest and wisest of his brothers, would find the golden bird without problem.

After he had journeyed just a short distance, he reached a forest. At the entrance to this forest, he saw a fox sitting out in the open, so he took his bow and arrow out and tried to shoot at it. The eldest son failed on first attempt but got ready to try again.

The fox, pleased with his good luck, turned to the boy and said, "Stop! Please do not shoot me, for I can offer you good advice. I know what you are looking for, and I can help you."

The boy stopped, put away his bow and arrow, and moved towards the strange creature. "By sunset, you will reach a village where there are two inns. You must stay in the poor, dirty one and no other," continued the fox.

The eldest son did not listen though and continued on his journey. When faced with his choice of lodgings, he did not choose the poor and dirty inn, as the fox had said. Instead, he chose the lively one. He entered and forgot all about the challenge and his country.

**1**

## What was special about the tree's fruit?

ⓐ It was made of gold.

ⓑ It was made of silver.

ⓒ It was made of bronze.

ⓓ It was made of platinum.

**2**

## Who saw the golden apple thief?

ⓐ The eldest son

ⓑ The gardener

ⓒ The youngest son

ⓓ The king

**3**

## What did the eldest son meet in the forest?

ⓐ A cat

ⓑ A fox

ⓒ A dog

ⓓ A rabbit

**4** What was stealing the golden apples?

ⓐ A man

ⓑ A bird

ⓒ A boy

ⓓ A woman

**5** What did the king insist upon having?

**6** What was the fox trying to offer the eldest son?

**Look at the following words and match each word on the left with a word on the right that has a similar meaning.**

Angry •                          • Selection

Amazement •                      • Wonder

Extraordinary •                  • Mad

Choice •                         • Amazing

**Read and circle which statements are true and which are false.** (True= ☺, False= ☹)

ⓐ The gardener had three sons.  ☺ ☹

ⓑ The youngest son was the gardener's favorite.  ☺ ☹

ⓒ The eldest son caught the golden apple thief.  ☺ ☹

ⓓ The youngest son went to get the golden bird first.  ☺ ☹

# 3 Complete and recite the summary below with words from the chapter. (10 words)

There once lived a king who had a very ① ____________

garden. In his garden, he had a tree that

② ____________ golden apples. One year, one of the

③ ____________ apples went missing. The ④ ____________

was very angry and asked the ⑤ ____________ to watch the

tree and to catch the thief. The gardener had three sons

and asked each of them in turn to take watch. The first

two sons failed, but the ⑥ ____________ son shot an arrow

at the golden bird that had been stealing the apples. He

presented the golden ⑦ ____________ to the king, and the

king then ⑧ ____________ that he must have the whole bird.

The ⑨ ____________ son set off on a quest to find the

bird and met a kind fox who gave him ⑩ ____________ .

# Chapter 2

# Taking Good Advice

Time passed, and, as no word was heard about the eldest son, the gardener sent out his second son. He hoped that his second son would at least return. The second son was a lot like his elder brother — confident and foolish — because when he too met the fox on the edge of the forest, he too did not heed the animal's words of advice.

On arrival at the village and faced with the choice of entering the lively, fun, luxurious inn or the poor and dirty inn, he said to himself, "I would be a fool not to go into the lively and luxurious inn as who in their right mind would even consider entering the other?"

So he followed in his brother's footsteps and ignored the fox's advice. He too entered the inn of luxury and forgot all about the golden bird, his father, and his country.

As even more time passed and his two older sons did not return, the gardener knew that at some point he might have to send out his youngest and favorite boy. The youngest had been wishing for that very moment as he was desperate to venture out into the big wide world on an adventure to please the king and to make his father proud. However, as ill-fortune had clearly fallen on his two older sons, the gardener grew more and more reluctant to let his youngest son go. Nevertheless, at last he had to allow him to go.

**Word Study**

at least    confident    foolish    edge    heed    luxurious    footstep    desperate
venture    ill fortune    reluctant

**Key Expression**

*On* arrival at the village and faced with the choice of entering the lively, fun, luxurious inn or the poor and dirty inn.

So, the youngest of the three sons set off on his quest and, like his brothers before him, met the fox at the edge of the forest, where he heard the same advice. However, while his brothers had disregarded the fox's words, the youngest listened and made no attempt on the fox's life.

In response, the fox continued, "Sit upon my tail, dear boy, and you will travel faster to your destination."

So the youngest son sat down on the fox's tail, and away they went through the forest and over the mountains so quickly that their hair whistled in the wind.

**Word Study**

quest    disregard    destination    whistle

**Key Expression**

So the youngest son sat down on the fox's tail, and away they went through the forest and over the mountains **so** quickly **that** their hair whistled in the wind.

Finally, the fox and the youngest son arrived at the same village with the two inns. Without even looking at the fancy one, the youngest brother went immediately to the poor and dirty one and rested there all night. He had already achieved what his brothers hadn't. His mind was still on the challenge, and when he awoke, he was excited to continue.

As he was beginning to continue his journey, the fox came to greet him with some further words of wisdom.

"Now, young man, listen to me once again as I have some more advice for you concerning your quest. Go straight until you reach the castle on the

**Word Study**

rest   achieve   challenge   wisdom   troop   snore   ignore   regret

**Key Expression**

**Without** even look**ing** at the fancy one, the youngest brother went immediately to the poor and dirty one.

other side of the forest. There, lying in wait, are a troop of soldiers who are fast asleep and snoring. Ignore them and go immediately into the castle. Pass room after room until you come to the room where the golden bird sits in a wooden cage. Do not try to take the golden bird out of the wooden cage and place her in the golden cage that sits very close by, or you will regret it!"

The young boy had listened carefully, and the fox hoped that he would again heed his advice.

As the young boy sat on the fox's tail, he wondered to himself about his brothers, where they were, and why they had failed where he had succeeded. But he did not have much time to think because the fox traveled so fast that they were, within no time at all, in front of the castle gates.

"I can go no further, my friend. Remember the advice I gave you and bring out the bird in the shabby wooden cage," said the fox again.

"I will," smiled the young man.

He slowly made his way through the castle gates and was slightly startled to see all the soldiers lying sleeping when they should have been on guard. He quickly but quietly made his way past them as he was afraid that one might wake up and find him there. Once inside the castle walls, the youngest son made his way past several large castle rooms, but none contained the golden bird. It wasn't until he reached the furthest room at the end of the longest corridor that he came upon the chamber that was holding the golden bird.

He entered the chamber, and, by the light from the window, he could see the golden bird sitting peacefully in its wooden cage. Next to it stood the cage of pure gold, and in that were the three golden apples that the golden bird had taken from the king's garden.

**Word Study**

wonder    succeed    shabby    slightly    startled    corridor    chamber

**Key Expression**

*Once* inside the castle walls, the youngest son made his way past several large castle rooms.

The young boy stood and thought to himself, 'It would be a very sad thing to carry such a fine bird away in such a tattered cage.'

So instead of remembering the fox's advice, he took hold of the beautiful bird and placed her in the golden cage. This was a huge mistake because the bird let out such a loud scream when he moved her that she awoke all of the soldiers, who then took the young man prisoner and carried him before their king. It was decided that he would be sentenced to death unless he could bring the king a golden horse that galloped as swiftly as the wind. Then, and only then, would his life be spared and the golden bird be given to him to keep. The young boy had been given a second chance.

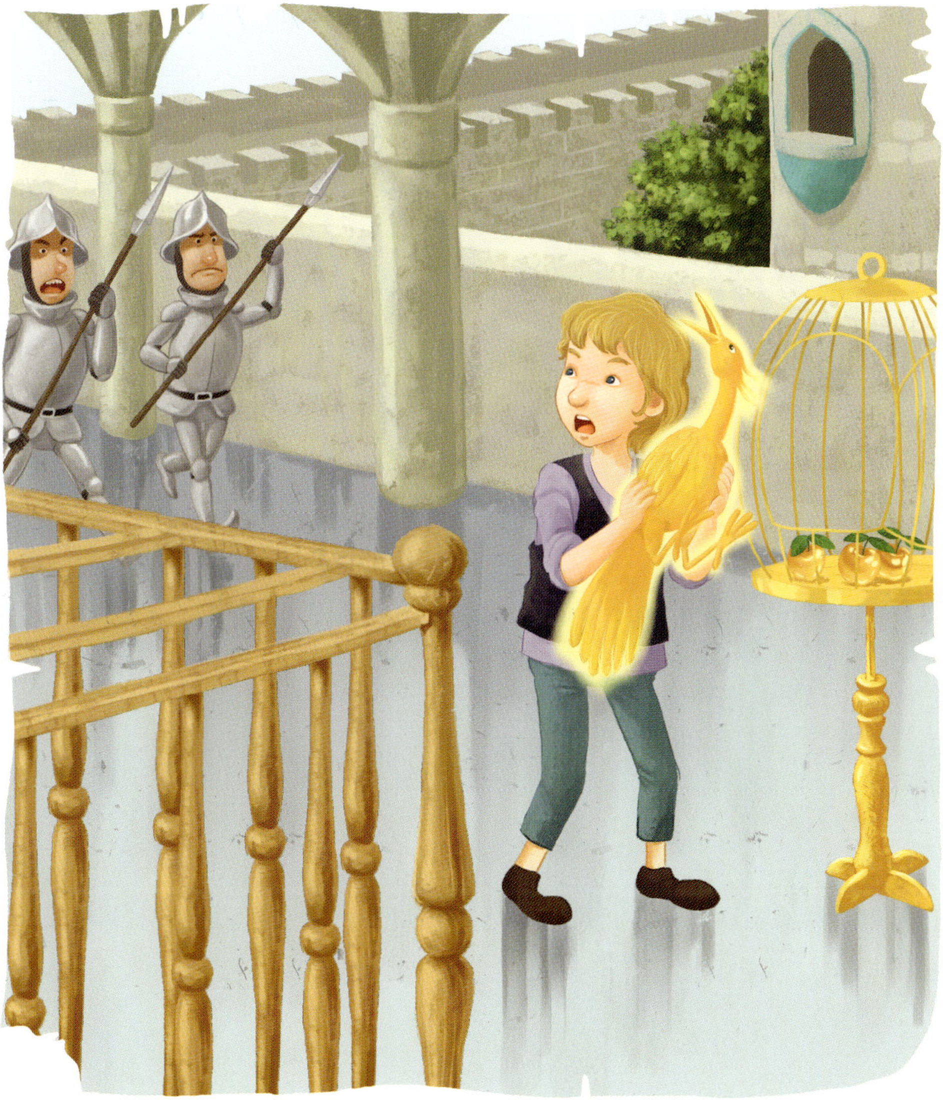

scream   awake   prisoner   sentence   gallop   swiftly   spare



It would be a very sad thing to carry **such a fine bird** away in such a tattered cage.

## 1

**What had the youngest son been wishing for?**

ⓐ A job

ⓑ A new bike

ⓒ A girlfriend

ⓓ An adventure

## 2

**Who would be lying in wait at the castle?**

ⓐ Nothing

ⓑ A gang of men

ⓒ A fleet of horses

ⓓ A troop of soldiers

## 3

**Which cage did the fox tell the youngest son NOT to touch?**

ⓐ The silver one

ⓑ The bronze one

ⓒ The golden one

ⓓ The wooden one

**4** Where was the chamber with the golden bird?

**Which inn did the second son enter?**

**5**

**6** What mistake did the youngest son make?

## 1

**Look at the following words and match each word with a word that means the opposite.**

Foolish •                          • Poor

Luxurious •                        • Loudly

Peacefully •                       • Wise

Shabby •                           • Elegant

## 2

**Read and circle which statements are true and which are false.** (True= ☺, False= ☹)

ⓐ The youngest son always listened to the fox.   ☺  ☹

ⓑ The youngest son longed for adventure.   ☺  ☹

ⓒ The second son was also confident and foolish.   ☺  ☹

**Read the two summaries and decide which is better for this chapter. Then recite the summary.**

ⓐ

The youngest son set out on the quest to get the golden bird and also met the fox on the edge of the forest. However, the youngest son listened to the fox's advice and stayed in the poor inn. The youngest son then left the village and traveled to the castle where the golden bird was. As the fox had advised, the boy went into the castle and took the bird without changing the cage that it was in. He had completed the quest and went home.

ⓑ

The youngest son set out on the quest to get the golden bird, and, unlike his brothers, when he met the fox, he listened to the advice he was given. On the way to the castle where the golden bird could be found, the fox offered some further advice to the youngest son. However, he did not take this advice, so the son was caught by the castle guards and taken before the king to be punished.

# Chapter 3

# Second, Third, and Fourth Chances

The youngest son had been blessed with a second chance despite the fact that he had clearly ignored the wise counsel that the fox had given him. So, once more, he set out on a journey and a quest, but this time it was to save his life. However, the young man was not as happy and confident this time around.

He walked and sighed, and then, suddenly, the wise fox appeared before him and said, "Do you now see what happens when you don't listen to my advice?"

"Yes," the youth replied with his head down in shame. "I should have listened to you. If I had, I would be at home now with my father, and my king would have his golden bird. I am sorry, Mr. Fox."

Despite the fox's disappointment, he felt that the young man had learned his lesson, so he decided to help him once more on his mission.

"This time, young man, your life depends upon you listening and heeding my advice," the fox said while the boy nodded.

"The golden horse stands in a stable to the back of the castle on the east side of the kingdom. By the horse's side will lie a groom, who, like the soldiers, will be fast asleep. You must quietly lead the horse out of the stable while it is wearing the old leather saddle and not the golden one that sits close by. Do you understand?"

**Word Study**

be blessed with    sigh    appear    shame    mission    depend upon    stable
groom    leather    saddle

**Key Expression**

I *should have listened* to you.

The boy nodded again and assured the fox
that this time he would not fail. The fox then stretched
out his tail once again and took the boy to where he
needed to go so quickly that his hair whistled in the
wind.

Like many times before when the fox's advice had been correct, there in the stable next to the golden horse lay a groom sound asleep and snoring. Then came the moment of truth: Had the youngest son learned his lesson, he would either remember the fox's instructions and place the worn leather saddle on the back of the horse and lead him out, or he would be too impressed by the shining gold saddle that lay close by.

**Word Study**

nod    assure    stretch out    correct    sound asleep    impress    shining

**Key Expression**

*Had* the youngest son *learned* his lesson, he would either remember the fox's instructions.

'What a great pity to put a worn and tattered leather saddle onto the back of such a beautiful creature. He deserves only the best, and I can give that to him,' he thought.

With that thought, the boy stretched out his

arms and lifted the golden saddle off the wall. As he did so, the guard began to wake up and let out an almighty scream to alert the other guards that an intruder was in the stall. Soon, the youngest son was surrounded once more by guards and was taken prisoner.

The next morning, the boy was again taken before the court to be judged, and yet again he was sentenced to death. However, like before, the court set a condition: If the boy could bring before them a beautiful princess, not only would his life be spared but he would also have the horse and the bird for his own.

**Word Study**

pity    tattered    lift    almighty    intruder    stall    set a condition

**Key Expression**

*What a great pity to* put a worn and tattered leather saddle onto the back of such a beautiful creature.

The young man set out again. This time his heart and mind were filled with sorrow. He had come so close to achieving his missions but then failed. As the young boy was contemplating these thoughts, the old, wise fox came up beside him and said, "You failed because once again you did not listen to the advice that I gave you. But as I am a kind old fox, I will help you again and help you find the princess." The young boy looked at the fox and smiled. He didn't need to say thank you as his facial expression said everything.

"Follow this road straight, and by dusk you will reach a beautiful castle. At twelve o'clock, the princess takes her evening bath. If you approach her and give her a kiss on the cheek, she will allow you to lead her away. Do not ask her parents for their permission; simply lead her out of the castle. Do you understand?"

The boy promised the fox that he did, so, like before, the fox offered the boy his tail, and the two traveled straight to the castle.

The fox and the young man reached the castle just in time, and the boy met the princess on the way to her bath and gave her a kiss. As the fox had said, the princess agreed to run away with him, but she begged that he take her before her parents and ask for permission. At first, the boy refused, but the princess wept and wept and fell to his feet till he could not take it anymore and gave in to her demands.

**Word Study**

set out    sorrow    contemplate    facial expression    dusk    bath    permission    refuse

**Key Expression**

***Follow*** this road straight, ***and*** by dusk you will reach a beautiful castle.

She led him up to her father's quarters, where the guards awoke and immediately took him into custody. He was a prisoner once again.

He was presented to the king that very night, and the king told him, "You will never have my daughter unless, within the next eight days, you can dig away the hill that stops the view from my window."

The young man had to accept the king's

challenge, but this hill was so big that there was no way he could do it by himself. After seven days of manual labor, the boy was exhausted and had achieved very little. Then, in his darkest hour, the old fox came alongside him and said, "Lie down and rest; I will work for you."

The boy slept through the night, and when he awoke, the hill was gone. The gardener's young son presented himself before the king and proudly said, "The hill is gone, your highness, and your view is clear." The king was obliged to keep his word and presented the young man with his daughter. Finally, the youngest son had achieved something.

**1**

**What did the youngest son need to ignore this time?**

ⓐ A golden bird

ⓑ A golden cage

ⓒ A golden saddle

ⓓ A golden princess

**2**

**What does the princess do at twelve o'clock?**

ⓐ Bathe

ⓑ Sleep

ⓒ Dance

ⓓ Eat

**3**

**How many days did the youngest son have to dig the hill away?**

ⓐ One

ⓑ Four

ⓒ Eight

ⓓ Twelve

**What did the princess beg for?**

ⓐ To eat some food

ⓑ To give her a kiss

ⓒ To give her a golden horse

ⓓ To ask her parents for permission

**Why did the fox decide to help the young man one more time?**

**Why did the boy think there was no way he could dig away the hill?**

## 1

**Look at the following words and match each word on the left with a word on the right that has a similar meaning.**

Stable •  　　　　• Positive

Confident •  　　　　• Stall

Ignore •  　　　　• Reject

Refuse •  　　　　• Disregard

## 2

**Read and circle which statements are true and which are false.** (True= ☺, False= ☹)

ⓐ The golden horse was in a stable.　☺　☹

ⓑ The youngest son was given a second chance.　☺　☹

ⓒ The youngest son dug away the hill by himself.　☺　☹

ⓓ The fox was kind and always helped.　☺　☹

**Complete and recite the summary below with words from the chapter.** (10 words)

The youngest son was given a ① _____________ chance to

② _____________ his life. When he left the ③ _____________ in

search of the ④ _____________ horse, he was not as

⑤ _____________ as before. Then the fox ⑥ _____________

again, and although he was ⑦ _____________ with the

youngest son, he also felt that the boy had learned his

⑧ _____________ . So the fox helped him again. However,

not once, but twice more, the young man did not

⑨ _____________ to the fox's advice and was captured by

guards. Finally, the young man listened to the fox and won

the ⑩ _____________ as the king had promised.

# Chapter 4

# The Last Challenge

As the young man walked away with the beautiful princess, the old fox approached and said, "We can have all three — the princess, the horse, and the bird."

"How?", begged the young man, thinking about how great that would be. The girl was very beautiful, and the young man could see himself getting married and settling down with this girl.

"If you will only listen to what I say, it will all be yours," said the fox as he rolled his eyes at the young man. "I will this time. I will listen and do only as you say," the young man promised.

**Word Study**

approach    get married    settle down    roll

**Key Expression**

"How?", begged the young man, ***thinking*** about how great that would be.

So the fox shared his advice once again,

"When you present yourself to the king and he asks for the beautiful princess, you must say, 'Here she is!' When he presents you with the horse, mount the horse. Then shake hands and say your goodbyes. Be sure to take the princess's hand last, and when you do, lift her up on to the horse, clap your heels, and gallop away as fast as you can."

This time, the boy didn't simply nod his head in agreement. He asked the fox to repeat his instructions once again so that he was sure of exactly what he needed to do. The fox did, and then the three companions went on their merry way.

**Word Study**

companion   merry   court   ride away   secure   fetch   inspect   securely   willingly

**Key Expression**

*It* was now *time to* secure the final item.

All went exactly to plan at the king's court; the young man rode away with the princess and the horse. It was now time to secure the final item: the golden bird, the very reason for the whole adventure.

"When you arrive at the castle where the bird is, the princess and I will remain outside. You must ride in and present the horse. As soon as the king sees you, he will fetch the bird and present it to you. But you must sit still and say that you wish to inspect the bird to be sure that it is the true golden bird. Once you have it securely in your hand, ride away as fast as you can," the fox advised once more. Again, the youth asked for the instructions to be repeated, and the fox did so willingly.

Finally, the princess, the horse, and the bird were secured, and the successful party rode into the great forest on their way home. Now the fox asked something of the young boy.

"Please cut off my head and feet and leave me here," the fox said, but the boy refused to do this awful thing, so the fox gave the boy his last piece of advice.

"Beware of two things: first, save no man from being sentenced to death; and, second, do not sit upon the bank of any river."

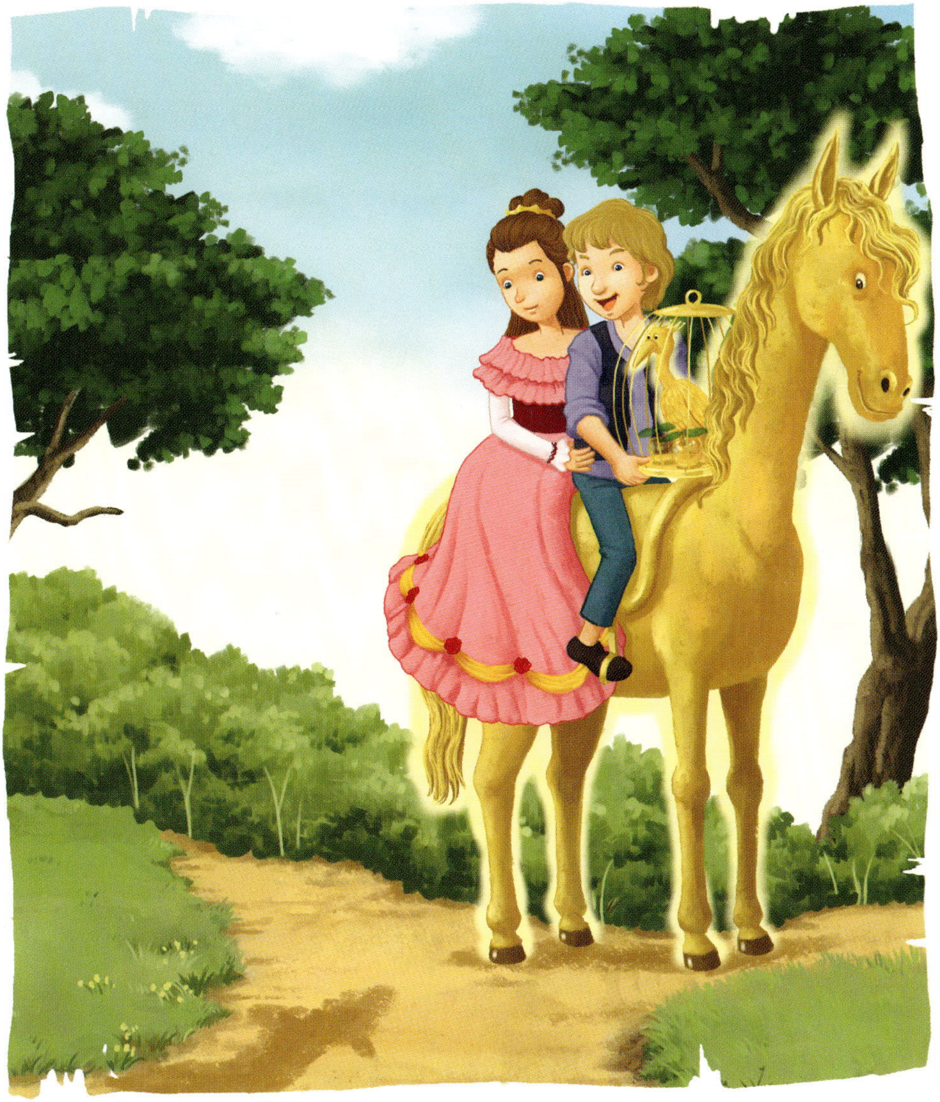

**Word Study**

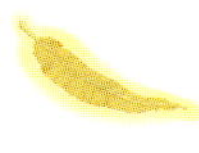

successful    cut off    awful    bank

**Key Expression**

Beware of two things***: first,*** save no man from being sentenced to death; and, ***second,*** do not sit upon the bank of any river.

With those words, the fox disappeared. The young man rode with the princess until they reached the village where he had spent his first night. The village was filled with a great noise and uproar. And when the boy asked the village folk what was going on, the people said, "Two men are going to be hanged!"

As the boy and his princess rode closer toward the village center, he realized that the two men about to be hanged were his brothers. For their freedom, the youngest brother had to give the village all his money. Now with his two brothers and the princess, they left the village for the journey home.

As they approached the edge of the forest, where each boy had first met the fox, the two older brothers insisted that they take a rest along the bank of a river to eat and to drink. In his hunger, the younger brother forgot the fox's last words of advice and said, "Yes, what a lovely idea!" He sat down next to his princess and, suspecting nothing, began to eat and drink when suddenly he felt a mighty push, and he fell down the bank of the river.

The two older boys then took the princess, the horse, and the bird and went home to their father and presented their trophies to the king.

The kingdom rejoiced, but the horse refused to eat, the bird would not sing, and the princess wept and wept.

Meanwhile, the youngest brother was forced to lie on the bottom of the river since he didn't have the strength to pull himself out. Just then, the wise, old fox reappeared and scolded the young boy for again not listening to his advice. However, the fox was too kind to leave the boy there; instead, he told the boy to hold on to his tail and then pulled him out of the river onto the bank where he had sat before.

"Your brothers will not allow you back into the kingdom, so you must disguise yourself," said the fox.

**Word Study**

rejoice    meanwhile    reappear    scold    disguise oneself    secretly

**Key Expression**

The horse refused to eat, the bird ***would not*** sing, and the princess wept and wept.

So the young man dressed like a poor working man and secretly walked straight into the king's court. He had only been there a moment when the horse began to eat, the bird began to sing, and the princess stopped weeping. The gardener's youngest son then explained the entire story to the king, who immediately banished the two evil older brothers from his kingdom.

After many years, when the young man, who was now a prince, and the princess were walking once again out by the edge of the forest, the fox came and begged the prince to take his life. This time, the prince did not argue. When he came to kill the kind old fox, the fox turned into a man. He was the brother of the princess and had been lost so many years before.

Word Study
moment    entire    banish    evil    argue

Key Expression
The bird **began to sing**, and the princess **stopped weeping**.

**1**

**What was the reason for the whole adventure?**

ⓐ The princess

ⓑ The golden horse

ⓒ The golden cage

ⓓ The golden bird

**Who was the fox?**

ⓐ The princess's sister

ⓑ The princess's father

ⓒ The princess's brother

ⓓ The princess's servant

**What did the youngest son have to give the village?**

ⓐ His bird

ⓑ His horse

ⓒ His money

ⓓ The princess

**3**

**4** What did the fox ask the youngest son?

**5** What did the youngest son promise to do when he went to take the horse and the bird again?

**6** What happened when the older brothers presented their trophies?

**Look at the following words and match each word on the left with a word on the right that has a similar meaning.**

Agreement •

• Later on

Willingly •

• Reluctantly

Scolde •

• Disagreement

Immediately •

• Praise

**Read and circle which statements are true and which are false.** (True= ☺, False= ☹)

ⓐ The young boy got all three prizes.
☺ ☹

ⓑ The fox was an old man.
☺ ☹

ⓒ The youngest son died.
☺ ☹

**Read the two summaries and decide which is better for this chapter. Then recite the summary.**

ⓐ

The youngest son finally listened to the fox's advice and walked away with all three prizes. The fox then gave him the last piece of advice: not to save those that were going to die and not to sit by the bank of a river. The youngest son learned his lesson, and this time he listened to everything the fox said. He traveled straight home and presented his prizes to the king. His father was very proud.

ⓑ

The youngest son walked away with the horse, the bird, and the princess. The fox advised him again: not to help those that were about to die and not to sit upon a river bank. In fact, the men that were about to die were his brothers, so he ignored the fox and helped them. He then sat down by a river bank, where his brothers pushed him into the river and stole his prizes. Luckily, however, he could go home thanks to the fox's help and tell the truth to the king.

**1** Who is/are the main character(s) in this story?

**2** Are any of the main characters like you or like somebody you know? What makes you think so?

**3** Describe your favorite character in this story and tell me why the character is your favorite.

**4** When do you think this story takes place? Where do you think this story takes place? Why do you think so?

**5** What is the funniest/ scariest/best part of this story?

**6** Is there a problem in this story?
If so, how does the problem get solved?
How would you have solved the problem?

**7** Would any of your friends/family enjoy this story? Why or why not?

**8** Could you come up with another good title for this story? What would it be?

**9** If you could change the ending of this story, what would it be?

**10** Do you think this story would make a good movie? Why or why not?

King 1

"Who would dare take one of my golden apples?"

The youngest son

"I will do a good job, Father. I promise I will catch the golden apple thief."

"But one feather is no good to me, men. I insist on having the entire bird!"

Fox

"Stop! Please do not shoot me, for I can offer you good advice. I know what you are looking for, and I can help you."

"By sunset, you will reach a village where there are two inns. You must stay in the poor, dirty one and no other."

Second son

"I would be a fool not to go into the lively and luxurious inn as who in their right mind would even consider entering the other?"

"Sit upon my tail, dear boy, and you will travel faster to your destination."

"Now, young man, listen to me once again as I have some more advice for you concerning your quest. Go straight until you reach the castle on the other side of the forest."

"There, lying in wait, are a troop of soldiers who are fast asleep and snoring. Ignore them and go immediately into the castle."

"Pass room after room until you come to the room where the golden bird sits in a wooden cage."

"Do not try to take the golden bird out of the wooden cage and place her in the golden cage that sits very close by, or you will regret it!"

"I can go no further, my friend. Remember the advice I gave you and bring out the bird in the shabby wooden cage."

"I will."

"It would be a very sad thing to carry such a
fine bird away in such a tattered cage."

"Do you now see what happens when you
don't listen to my advice?"

"Yes. I should have listened to you. If I had,
I would be at home now with my father,
and my king would have his golden bird. I am
sorry, Mr. Fox."

"This time, young man, your life depends
upon you listening and heeding my advice."

"The golden horse stands in a stable to the
back of the castle on the east side of the
kingdom. By the horse's side will lie a groom,
who, like the soldiers, will be fast asleep.

"You must quietly lead the horse out of the
stable while it is wearing the old leather
saddle and not the golden one that sits
close by. Do you understand?"

"What a great pity to put a worn and tattered leather saddle onto the back of such a beautiful creature. He deserves only the best, and I can give that to him."

"You failed because once again you did not listen to the advice that I gave you. But as I am a kind old fox, I will help you again and help you find the princess."

"Follow this road straight, and by dusk you will reach a beautiful castle. At twelve o'clock, the princess takes her evening bath.

"If you approach her and give her a kiss on the cheek, she will allow you to lead her away. Do not ask her parents for their permission; simply lead her out of the castle. Do you understand?"

King 2

"You will never have my daughter unless, within the next eight days, you can dig away the hill that stops the view from my window."

"Lie down and rest; I will work for you."

"The hill is gone, your highness, and your view is clear."

"We can have all three—the princess, the horse, and the bird."

"How?"

"If you will only listen to what I say, it will all be yours"

"I will this time. I will listen and do only as you say."

"When you present yourself to the king and he asks for the beautiful princess, you must say, 'Here she is!' When he presents you with the horse, mount the horse.

"Then shake hands and say your goodbyes. Be sure to take the princess's hand last, and when you do, lift her up on to the horse, clap your heels, and gallop away as fast as you can."

"When you arrive at the castle where the bird is, the princess and I will remain outside. You must ride in and present the horse."

"As soon as the king sees you, he will fetch the bird and present it to you. But you must sit still and say that you wish to inspect the bird to be sure that it is the true golden bird."

"Once you have it securely in your hand, ride away as fast as you can,"

"Please cut off my head and feet and leave
me here."

"Beware of two things: first, save no man
from being sentenced to death; and, second,
do not sit upon the bank of any river."

"Your brothers will not allow you back into
the kingdom, so you must disguise yourself,"

## Chapter 1  After Reading  p.20

1  ⓐ

2  ⓒ

3  ⓑ

4  ⓑ

5  He insisted on having the entire bird.

6  The fox was tried to offer advice.

## Chapter 1  Activities  p.22

1  Angry - Mad
Amazement - Wonder
Extraordinary - Amazing
Choice - Selection

2  ⓐ ☺
   ⓑ ☺
   ⓒ ☹
   ⓓ ☹

3  ① special
   ② bore
   ③ golden
   ④ king
   ⑤ gardener
   ⑥ youngest
   ⑦ feather
   ⑧ insisted
   ⑨ eldest
   ⑩ advice

## Chapter 2  After Reading  p.36

1  ⓓ

2  ⓓ

3  ⓒ

4  at the end of the longest corridor

5  He entered the luxurious inn.

6  He tried to place the golden bird in the golden cage.

## Chapter 2  Activities  p.38

1  Foolish - Wise
Luxurious - Poor
Peacefully - Loudly
Shabby - Elegant

2  ⓐ ☹
   ⓑ ☺
   ⓒ ☺

3  ⓑ

**Chapter 3  After Reading**  p.52

1  ⓒ

2  ⓐ

3  ⓒ

4  ⓓ

5  Because the fox felt the young man had learned his lesson.

6  Because the hill was too big.


**Chapter 3  Activities**  p.54

1  Stable - Stall
Confident - Positive
Ignore - Disregard
Refuse - Reject

2  ⓐ ☺
   ⓑ ☺
   ⓒ ☹
   ⓓ ☺

3  ① second
   ② save
   ③ castle
   ④ golden
   ⑤ confident
   ⑥ appeared
   ⑦ disappointed
   ⑧ lesson
   ⑨ listen
   ⑩ princess

**Chapter 4  After Reading**  p.70

1  ⓓ

2  ⓒ

3  ⓒ

4  The fox asked to take his life by cutting off his head and feet.

5  He promised to listen and do only as the fox said.

6  The horse refused to eat, the bird would not sing, and the princess kept on weeping.


**Chapter 4  Activities**  p.72

1  Agreement - Disagreement
Willingly - Reluctantly
Scolde - Praise
Immediately - Later on

2  ⓐ ☺
   ⓑ ☹
   ⓒ ☹

3  ⓑ